Tinder Dating

The Ultimate Beginner's Guide to Experiencing Success on Tinder

Table of Contents

Introduction

Tinder is the current buzzword in the dating world. Even celebrities like Britney Spears, Hillary Duff, and Leonardo DiCaprio are using it. But, why are they? What is it about Tinder that makes it suddenly cool to be on a dating app?

In this short, concise book, we will go over the history of Tinder, the science behind online dating, and how Tinder compares to other similar online dating vehicles. Most importantly, we will also briefly cover the pros and cons of using Tinder in one's everyday life.

While online dating and "hookup apps" are certainly a relatively new staple in the current state of the dating world, we must realize how to use these tools to our advantage and not to our detriment. By educating ourselves in regards to how to optimally use these tools and how to taper our expectations, we will be much happier in the long run.

The information here has been compiled from my own successes and failures, the experiences of others, and extensive research on the topic. I hope you can learn a thing or two in this book to avoid some of the common pitfalls!

Chapter 1:

What is Tinder?

As the dating world has continued to change along with technological advancements, Tinder is currently the fastest growing dating app in the world. In only a few years, the user count has reached close to 50 million unique members from all over the world. There are millions of new users joining each week.

Basics of Tinder

Tinder is a dating app that uses personal details submitted by its users. The app creates matches based on this information and then presents a roster of photos of other Tinder members. Matches are made based on mutual likes (based on the user's Facebook profile) and proximity. The user's preferences, including preferred age and gender of potential matches, are also bases for the app.

When the image of a "match" appears, the user can either swipe left or right based on how attractive/interesting they find that match. The basis for either swiping right (liking the person) or swiping left (rejecting a potential match) is largely based on looks but also partially based on characteristics, such as adventurousness or friendliness, as portrayed in the pictures. If a user likes a photo and then that person also liked the original user's photo, a match is made. Because of this, a user won't know if other users liked their photo unless a match is made.

Once a match is made, both parties will be able to open a chat box. From here, they can start conversing and eventually build a connection, and they can even set up an actual meeting.

Basics of Tinder

Tinder uses a Facebook profile as its main basis. Photos, page likes, posts to their account and other available information is gathered, creating a social graph. The app, then, analyzes the graph and compares it to that of other users in their system. Similar social graphs are made available to the user.

These profiles, particularly the profile photos, are visible to the user. Compatibility on Tinder is based on the geographic location of the users, common interests and mutual friends.

The basic features of Tinder include the following:

Swipe is the central Tinder feature, which practically dictates the ultimate outcome. There are two swipes a user makes: a "swipe left" or a "swipe right."

A "swipe right" means the user likes the current photo. If that person happens to also swipe right on the user's photo, a match is made.

A "swipe left" means that the user is not interested in the person. This will remove that person from the list of potential matches and will then open another photo. A user can keep swiping left to keep searching the database. However, once a photo is swiped left, there is no turning back.

Moments

Tinder Moments is a recent update made available in June 2014. This is a photo feature that heavily resembles the popular Instagram app. Tinder Moments allows users to post pictures and wait for other users to like it. These photos are only up for 24 hours. Once beyond that time frame, the photo is automatically deleted.

People can only see and like the photos if they are matched with the person who posted them. Photos on Tinder Moments can also be edited, like in other photo sharing apps. Filters can also be added for enhancement. There are even options for adding drawings to the photos.

Chapter 2:

History of Tinder

Friends Sean Rad and Justin Mateen, together with Jonathan Badeen, founded Tinder in 2013. The app was developed at the University of Southern California and later was expanded to include other universities. Over the years, the app became available throughout the United States and then expanded into other countries as well.

Since it was initially offered, the membership has grown rapidly. Customer reviews were favorable, which earned Tinder the "Best New Startup of 2013" award in the Crunchie Awards by TechCrunch. Today, Tinder is available in several countries and in more than 30 languages. In some areas, Tinder users reach up to 10% of the entire population. The average time spent by most users is more than an hour every day.

The latest statistics show that in April of 2015, 26 million matches were made each day and that about 1.6 billion profiles on Tinder are swiped through each day. Perhaps even more impressive is that since its introduction in 2012, more than 6 billion matches have been made.

How Tinder Works

Part of Tinder's rapid success has been credited to how simple the app is to use. Furthermore, it only takes a few minutes to set up, removing the barrier of entry that some comprehensive dating applications require. Once registered on Tinder and an authentic Facebook profile is linked, the app immediately scans the entire Tinder database for anyone and everyone that can be a potential match.

It searches users that are within a predefined search area, such as within a one-mile radius from where the user is currently located. When a list of Tinder users nearby has been established, the profiles are then compared. Profiles that match the user's preferences are made accessible. Every Tinder user that corresponds to certain factors, such as in the following example, will be accessible:

Lives within 1 mile from the user (the app uses GPS to find the user's location)

Age is within a predefined range (e.g., all males 25-30 years old, 20-something single females, etc.)

Reasons for using Tinder are similar (e.g., looking for casual date, looking for single college students, looking for young professionals in the IT industry, etc.)

Aside from these basic factors, Tinder will check the user's Facebook profile to gather more data to further narrow down the list of potential matches. Nobody wants to have to scroll through hundreds of profiles only to get a handful of really interesting ones. Tinder wants to give a shorter roster of profiles that have a high probability for a match.

To do this, Tinder will check the "likes" on the user's Facebook profile. Any Tinder user, after satisfying the basic conditions in the example above, who also liked the same pages in their own Facebook profile, is included into the list of potential matches.

Each Tinder profile only includes very basic information, though nothing too personal. There is just a name (last names are optional), an age, a few pages liked on Facebook and, the most critical of all, a photo.

Despite all the trouble and detail the app uses in order to come up with a valid and useful roster, the ultimate decision still rests on its users. If one user swipes right and the other user swipes left back, a match is instantly made. They can start chatting and eventually meet up on their own terms.

Chapter 3:

The Science Behind Online Dating

Despite the huge success of Tinder, and some notable progress by other online dating apps, there are still quite a number of people who are apprehensive about this entire thing. In many ways, the system of online dating is pretty much the same as it is in the real world, just systematized and made easier.

Why Tinder Works

Dating, on the whole, is a very controversial subject, and online dating has been getting much heat over the past few years. Even the simplicity and freedom that apps like Tinder provide to its users, it is not without criticism.

First off, the truth of the matter is that a majority of Tinder users do base their swipes on profile photos. That's typically "judging the book by its cover." This is something that many people, particularly those with below-average looks, feel is a limitation with this service. In many peoples' eyes, Tinder is just another app that promotes shallow relationships in an already shallow society. While there is no doubt that looks do matter in relationships, whether in person or online, a topic like this is sure to be polarizing.

However, there are several psychological explanations as to why Tinder still reigns over other dating apps, despite massive opposition by some camps. In fact, Tinder has made online dating something of a trend. Before, a large percentage of people were ashamed to admit to using online dating sites and apps. With Tinder, however, there is a noticeable difference in the way its users are perceived by their peers. This case is certainly helped by the fact that many Hollywood celebrities have claimed that they use the service in their own personal lives.

Reason #1:

Tinder Is "Cool"

Tinder has an amazing marketing strategy. Historically, while most online dating sites and apps may be popular according to the numbers, users generally are not keen on telling their peers that they are on such platforms. In fact, many users would try to keep their usage of these apps a secret. Tinder has made it a goal to promote its service as a "hip" and "cool" thing to do. Users of other dating apps are still not as public with their usage, even though this is slowly changing.

Reason #2:

Instant Gratification

One of Tinder's greatest strengths lies in eliminating the lag in terms of time and distance. Because the available roster of potential matches is within close proximity, people can instantly meet their match in a matter of minutes. Most other dating apps and sites would take quite a few days before parties eventually meet in person. In most cases, distance becomes a huge obstacle in the success of online dating.

The typical story of most dating sites in the past would be that two users hit it off only to find it difficult to meet up in person. In this world with shortened attention spans and increasingly more options in our personal lives, instant gratification has become key to many marketing strategies. Delaying is losing opportunity. With Tinder, a person gets to invest time and effort in getting to know a person who is very much accessible. Think of this scenario:

Scene 1: Boy meets girl who lives across the country

The two hit it off, talking as though they have known each other for a long time. They make each other laugh. They agree on most things. Things just come naturally. What's the next step? Meet. But, then, there's the distance. These two would now spend their time planning and coordinating their schedules. Then there is the issue on transportation and cost. Time spent in planning the "Big Meet" also creates a bigger chance of cold feet in both parties.

Scene 2: Boy meets girl who lives 10 minutes away

The same thing happens. They chat. They hit it off. They make each other laugh. So, now they want to see each other in person. They give addresses or decide where they can both go for the "Big Meet." In less than 30 minutes, the two are sitting at a diner, talking and laughing in person. They are enjoying themselves in less than 24 hours from their first interaction.

Out of the two above scenarios, the second one is more attractive for most people. The momentum of finding someone, hitting it off, and establishing a real connection happens in a continuous process. This is crucial in this day and age where everything passes by so quickly. People, especially in their social life, have this need to take things as they come right then and there.

Waiting is no longer what most people are keen on doing. If something does not work out or there is no chemistry in the beginning stages, it is time to move on. This exact thinking is what Tinder uses to its advantage and what draws in so many users.

Aside from these two, there is still more to the psychology of why Tinder is as big of a success as it is today:

Hook-Ups

Truth be told, most of the top dating apps in the market are aimed as a way for people to hook-up. It may not be the first and foremost goal for everybody, but a lot of people eventually hook-up. However, with Tinder, hook-ups come in two different forms: cyber (online) hook-up and an actual hook-up. People have a choice whether to do the deed in person or do it over the Internet. Strange as it may sound to some, the idea of using hook-up apps is increasingly becoming more enticing compared to actually hooking up in person.

A few years ago, dating sites were a means to an end – an in person hook-up between the parties. Today, hooking up over the Internet is the end in itself. There are many reasons for this, which vary from person to person. Some may see it as a safe way of checking out if one is attractive enough. Some may use this to boost self-confidence or feel good about themselves. Some may just use this as a way to pass time. Others may use dating apps as a means of socializing but also as a way to avoid common awkwardness when socializing in person. Some may want casual hook-ups but are not up for going to the typical meeting locations such as a bar, nightclub, or coffee shop. There is obviously a wide range of reasons, sometimes overlapping, and Tinder is doing a great job of providing these solutions for people.

Specifically, the majority of Tinder users use the app with the goal of finding someone to hook up with, whether online or in person. A large percentage of these users find their satisfaction in "Tindering" rather than in the actual hook-up. The act of swiping through other people's profiles and seeing how many matches they make is an end goal in itself for some.

Digital Eligibility Over Physical Eligibility

One often overlooked factor in the online dating world (mainly for those who are less experienced with it), is that digital attractiveness is, more often than not, greater than the person's actual attractiveness. However, not all of the blame goes to the user who posted the picture, as we can also "fall" for a person's picture because of the amount of time we are able to look at it versus being labeled a "creep" if we were to stare at a person like that in a physical setting.

Nonetheless, this very real phenomenon has been proven countless times. In the digital world, anyone can be as attractive as they want to be. Anyone can place anything on his or her Facebook or Tinder profiles. A common, proven behavior is that people tend to post things that make them look witty, attractive, and delightful, which could cause another user could interpret these people as portraying these traits consistently in their daily life. In reality, the person could have spent a week concocting the perfect line and not have any ammunition left, so to say.

Nonetheless, photos can be carefully crafted to make one look astonishingly beautiful or attractively mysterious. Whether it is men rounding up their height or women rounding down their weight, Tinder has definitely used this interesting piece of psychology to their advantage when creating this revolutionary app.

Needs

Tinder satisfies society's growing social and evolutionary needs. People often think that technology changes behavior. A few realize that it is human behavior that tells what direction technology will take. Look at why and how social media has become such a phenomenal success. Tinder is able to provide the basic socialization and, at times sexual, needs. The manner is, at best, infantile, but it works anyways.

People have this innate need to be accepted, to be attractive. There is also an inner competitiveness in (most) people, which is nourished by one's dating potential. People are increasingly turning to dating apps to feed their need of self-assurance. On Tinder, users get immediate feedback on their dating potential. They can also quickly revise their profiles and get immediate feedback. They get to find out what can potentially make them attractive and what can turn people off.

Imitates Real Dating Scene

In many ways, Tinder is a lot like the in-person dating scene. For starters, Tinder can be used as a testing ground before committing to dating anyone. Despite the naysayers, Tinder has become an extension of real world dating in just a few years. It resembles the first steps to getting a date but eliminates a huge chunk of the awkwardness and obstacles that are typically involved.

Because the app searches its database of users to see who is most likely to hit it off, based on age and gender preferences, mutual friends and common interests, a great deal of the awkward dialogue is removed from play. With the assumption that the matches are already somewhat similar in their interests, users can jump straight into deciding who they feel is attractive.

In a way, setting up a Tinder profile is akin to getting dressed up for a night out. Once a profile is done and posted, the app then becomes a very efficient matchmaker. A person would not have to scout a roomful of people, trying hard to spot a potential date and, most of the time, failing miserably (of course this is an advantage for the more charismatic). How much time is spent in spotting potential dates, preparing one's self for an introduction, mustering enough courage to go up to that person, and introducing one's self? How many awkward, embarrassing moments occurred as a result from this random introduction?

Next, the app gives a push in the right direction to encourage communication. Once a match is made, people already have basic information about the other party. This is very crucial in the dating scene. It helps people know what topics to talk about, which eliminate uncomfortable silences or awkward comments when moving forward.

Simply put, Tinder streamlines a person's choices when it comes to dating. It also gives people enough of a glimpse into what the other person is like so they can decide if they are worth the time invested. Time is precious and Tinder definitely eliminates time-consuming preliminaries in the dating world, for better or worse.

More and more people are discovering that it is much easier, more convenient, and more rewarding to judge about a hundred Tinder profiles in less than five minutes and see potential matches than to go out and spend more than an hour assessing if one person can be a potential match. It's much like casting a net to catch more fish with a higher probability of success than using a time-consuming, less successful bait-and-tackle method to catch just one after spending considerable time.

Additionally, checking people out in a bar is similar to browsing through Tinder profiles. Yes, this process is on the superficial side, but that exists to some degree in all human beings with a healthy libido. Simply, people judge how others look. This is true not just in the dating scene but even in business relationships.

People sit next to others on a bus or train that they deem to be "safe" to share the ride with. Students often choose to sit next to students who look cool and interesting. People ask directions from someone who look nice and approachable. All of these did not require getting to know a person on a deeper level, as it all took judging by appearances.

Next, gauging interest. Once a person spots someone (at a party, bar, etc.), he/she pays closer attention and checks to see if anything interesting is going on with said person. In "Tinderworld," this is reading through one's profile to see any common interests or signs that a person might be worth pursuing even further.

Then comes the swipe. Swiping right or left is akin to either deciding to go up to a person or to turn away and find someone else. Swiping right is similar to walking towards the person to pursue further communication, while swiping left is similar to deciding that they aren't worth it.

The next part of the dating process is striking up a conversation. This is typically the pivotal point of an evening. If the two hit it off, then the encounter is likely to proceed. If not, then it's time to move on to the next person. On Tinder, this would be the chat. Whether Tinder purposely modeled its app off of the typical way in which people meet in the Western World is not certain, but the parallels seem to be endless.

Anonymity

For the most part, a person can be as anonymous as they'd like to on Tinder. They get to choose what to reveal, and this also allows for people to "edit" who they are. They can be anyone they want to be. This typically makes people more confident about themselves and the profile that they are portraying to their potential matches.

In some cases, this helps them to actually be more themselves - charming, assertive, or confident. A lot of people miss out on great conversations because they are so concerned about how they are perceived by others in a certain environment.

Chapter 4:

Effects of Using Tinder

Tinder has become an addictive past-time for many people, some spending so much time on Tinder that they might as well treat it as a part-time job (albeit one that doesn't pay any money). Ironically, this app came out at a time when many of these same people were "too busy" to go out and meet people the traditional way.

Nevertheless, for others, it has become a medium in which people can stay connected even while traveling or being stuck in their office at work. Because of its ability to potentially make someone's dating life more efficient, it is useful for a wide range of demographics, from teenagers in college to busy professionals.

However, even with all of this convenience, there are quite a few tangible effects seen from using Tinder. Some of these effects benefit users, while others are more detrimental than beneficial. It all boils down to how a person uses Tinder and for what reason. After all, just like with all other social media apps, Tinder is essentially a tool - one that can help you achieve your desired results.

Missing out on a potentially good match

Because there are so many available Tinder profiles, it is very tempting to keep swiping left. Again, once a "swipe left" is made, that "discarded" Tinder profile will no longer be available. However, because there is a chance of seeing more Tinder profiles, people easily dismiss profiles. The thinking here is that there might be a better match somewhere further along the roster of Tinder profiles or that maybe even the next day's roster will feature more interesting profiles.

Also, because of the promise of receiving more potential matches in the following days, some no longer commit enough time to chatting or getting to know the other person. Most are only willing to give a few minutes in chatting and then quickly dismiss the other person as uninteresting. Being superficial has just become more superficial. Again, this effect is highly dependent on the user. If the user really wants to find romance, then he/she should commit more time to studying profiles and engaging in deeper chat conversations. While this is individual, there is no doubt that Tinder is set up to encourage the idea of “plenty of fish in the sea.”

People are not always who they say they are

Because of the anonymity, user control, and privacy settings, people can practically tell all sorts of lies in this medium. People are not required to be wholly truthful with their profiles or even when they are chatting. It is very easy to bend some truths or even to create an elaborate lie.

There is a virtual mask for people to hide behind. Because they are not talking face-to-face, people have more courage to conjure up things that they wouldn't normally say while looking a person in his/her eyes. One can never be too sure if the person he/she liked on Tinder will still be as delightful and interesting in person or even look as promising as they had portrayed themselves to be.

Sadly, some users enjoy this effect. They find enjoyment in pretending to be someone else and seeing what type of reactions they can get. There are no strings attached to this behavior, so who cares if a totally average guy pretends to be the CEO of a huge tech company?

It is like a grownup version of playing pretend. Users must be cautioned, though, not to take everything at face value. Online, whether on dating apps or elsewhere (think: scammers), not everyone is exactly who they say they are. So, be wary. Enjoy your chats and certainly show interest when someone seems intriguing, but never get too wrapped up in the idea of someone until you meet them in person.

Chapter 5:

Pros And Cons of Tinder

Like most things in life, there is also an upside and a downside to Tinder use. These pros and cons depend heavily on personal views, opinions, preferences, and purpose, so here are the common ones:

Pros

It is quick to set up. In a few minutes, a Tinder profile can be created and potential matches are available. All it takes is a Facebook profile and few other details, such as name (user name), age, preferences, and interests on whom to meet and from where.

It is a lot like actual dating but less personal and more convenient for busy people, those who have some apprehensions about dating, or those who are self-conscious about themselves.

Mutual friends on Facebook increase successful matches. Much like in real life where a friend of a friend (and so on) is a potential date, Tinder knows that people who belong to the same social circles have a higher chance of hitting it off.

The app is designed originally for mobile devices, which makes it very easy to use. Stuck in line somewhere? Create a Tinder profile and who knows, someone interesting is sitting in a cab a few cars away from you. Better yet, stuck in a party? Open Tinder on a smartphone and a surprise might be waiting, as another guest at the party might be also bored and on Tinder right at that moment.

There is limited embarrassment. Because of the anonymity and no need for a face-to-face interaction, people find themselves less shy and more likely to interact (i.e. chat) more.

There are limited emails. Unlike most other dating apps in which almost anyone can send emails, Tinder only allows matches to send emails to each other. Any user that wasn't liked or did not like back will not be able to send emails to the user.

Cons

Some people may find it shallow because matches are almost always made based on the users' assessment of other users' photos. Again, judging a book by its cover is promoted in this medium.

Based on studies and observations, female users are more likely to start a conversation when matches are made. Males tend to just wait for a match to happen but are less likely start a chat.

The truth is, the majority of users are only on Tinder to look for casual hook-ups and not for a serious romantic relationship. The proximity of the matches makes this very convenient. However, there are still many couples that have developed strong relationships after meeting on Tinder.

It is highly addictive. Users compare it to Candy Crush and Facebook rolled into one, with a dash of sex thrown in. Be aware of the way you use your time, especially if you are neglecting other areas of your life in favor of this app. Think about this... If you know you want to drop a few pounds or study a little more, will the short term high you receive from chatting on Tinder be better than spending an hour a day building up your body and health, or studying to improve your future job prospects and earning power, which would inevitably make you a more valuable in the dating market anyway? There is certainly a balance that everyone must consider when it comes to improving themselves and accepting their current self.

Chapter 6:

Tinder Compared to Other Dating Sites

Tinder is not the only dating app available. It is one, however, if not the most popular of all dating apps in recent times. Let's explore two similar, yet different apps in the form of OKCupid and Happn:

Happn

Happn is an app that works a little differently than the two other leading apps. Proximity is the focus of Happn. That is, people consider they have more chances of actually liking someone who goes to the same bar or gig than someone who lives nearby but never frequents these places that the user goes to.

Happn is considered by some to have a better matching algorithm than Tinder. Matches are largely based on similar interests and common places users have been. It is like matching people who might have already crossed paths in the real world. Maybe they had attended the same concert sometime in the past or went to the same bar a few days ago.

In terms of location, Happn automatically scans GPS locations of other users within a preset 250-meter radius. Profiles of anyone on Happn, that the user has not crossed paths with, won't be made available, even if these people are also within the search area. For instance, even if there are ten guys within a 250-meter radius from where a girl is, their profiles won't show up if they hadn't been in places that the girl had been (i.e. did not go to the same school, didn't live in the same neighborhood, did not attend the same concert, didn't go to the same bar, etc.).

Profiles that do show up mean that these people had, at some point, crossed paths with the user. The user can see more of the profiles and learn more, see more photos, as well as secretly like their profiles. Secretly liking one's profile is much like bookmarking a page for later perusing. To make contact, a "charm" is sent, which costs real money. Relative to Tinder, users can chat for free after matches are made.

Also, one other issue about Happn is the scope of search. Some users think that the 250-meter is not much help at all. It is too wide and in a place where there are tons of people, so crossing someone's path might not be as valuable (i.e. Manhattan).

OK Cupid

OKCupid has been around longer than both Tinder and Happn and can be considered the veteran of the group. It may be older but it has kept up with the changes in the dating scene. The website has been up since 2004 and the mobile app was introduced just five years ago.

OK Cupid works by asking 21 questions to each user. Answers will be used as basis for searching through a huge pool of users in order to make matches. The algorithm used for this is widely considered to be top notch, which makes the matches closely accurate.

This app does not utilize proximity features like Happn or the hip appeal of Tinder. OKCupid is more for people who are serious about dating, and for those who really want help in finding someone that they can have a real, deep relationship with and not a superficial one or a casual hook-up. Well, that is the focus of the service anyway.

Conclusion

Thank you for reading through this book. Dating apps are now increasingly becoming “the way to date”. Like most other endeavors, online dating carries its own risks. Do take care and be cautious. Having fun does not mean abandoning safety and societal norms necessarily.

Tinder works for a lot of people, especially those who are in it to have fun. It can also work for people who are looking for serious, long-term relationships. It just takes more time, effort, focus, and commitment.

Nevertheless, Tinder is a great dating app that singles must try at least once. Who knows? Maybe using it will lead you to your own successful love story.

I hope you were able to learn a thing or two from this book. Good luck on your own journey!

CPSIA information can be obtained
at www.ICGtesting.com
Printed in the USA
LVOW13s1630301117
558160LV00011B/656/P